DON HINSON

Discovering
Walks in Lakeland
Mountains

SHIRE PUBLICATIONS LTD

Contents

NOTE: the last figure in brackets is the total height climbed in feet (1ft is 0.3048m).

Maps are based on Ordnance Survey maps with the permission of the Controller of Her Majesty's Stationery Office, Crown copyright reserved.

The cover photograph was taken on the walk to Coniston Old Man.

Copyright © 1985 by Don Hinson. First published 1985. Number 277 in the Discovering series. ISBN 0 85263 717 9.

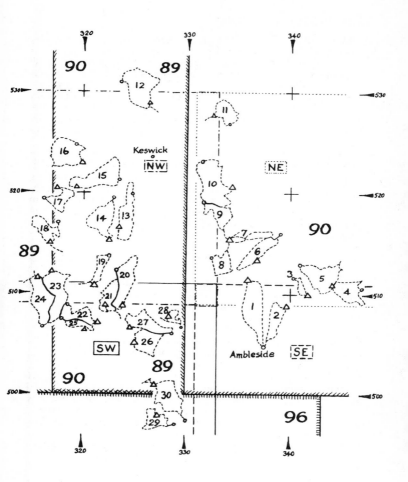

Map showing locations of all the walks
Circle = start. Triangle = highest peak reached. Shaded straight
lines = edges of Ordnance Survey 1:50,000 (1¼inch) maps
(numbers 89, 90 and 96). Plain straight lines = edges of
Ordnance Survey 1:25,000 (2½inch) maps: NW (dot-dash), NE
(dots), SW (solid line), SE (dashes).

Introductory notes

How to follow a route. A 1 or 1¼ inch to the mile map and a compass should be taken on walks. Before using this book, browse through the glossary to get an idea of the meaning of the words used in describing the route. Note: 'up' and 'down' always refer to gradients (unlike everyday speech, where you may go 'down' a level road). When choosing a walk, read the summary to get some idea whether it is suitable to your tastes and the weather. Get to know the shortest way back so that if caught by bad weather you know what to do without fumbling about with maps in rain or wind.

Some easier walks for beginners. 11 Blencathra, omitting the walk along the top (6,7) and Bannerdale Crags (10-14). (7½km, 4¾mi, 2200ft). **19** The Gables, omitting Great Gable by turning back to 7, then carrying on along to 15, etc (7½km, 4½mi, 1700ft). **21** Sty Head. No peaks climbed, but a fine walk in rugged surroundings. See last paragraph of summary. **29** Coniston Old Man shortened as in summary.

Glossary

Arete: narrow rocky ridge.

Cairn: pile of stones about 0.5m or so high to mark a path, fork in path, or viewpoint.

Col: top of a pass, where the ground is saddle shaped.

Drive: track leading to a private house or farm.

Farmgate: gate wide enough for vehicles to go through.

Fire break: wide treeless gap in plantation.

Lane: small surfaced public road.

On: keep walking in about the same direction.

Outcrop: mass of rock jutting out of ground.

Path: a way too narrow for vehicles.

Peak bagger: walker whose main aim is to climb (or 'bag') as many summits as possible.

Scramble: a climb (or descent) where careful walkers use hands as well as feet. Often rocky, but ropes etc are not needed.

Scree: an awful lot of small rocks (a few inches across). Bad to walk on, especially if they slip.

Stile: device helping walkers to climb over or through a hedge, fence or wall; the usual step need not be present.

Tarn: mountain pond.

Tongue: small ridge between two streams which meet at its bottom.

Track: a way wide enough for vehicles.

Abbreviations

E,S,N,W: east, south, north, west.

km, mi: kilometre, mile.

L: turn left through about 90°. But 'fork L' means take the left hand of two paths at a fork. This need not involve turning 90°.

4

half L: turn left through about 45°.

one-third L: turn left through about 30°.

two-thirds L: turn left through about 60°.

sharp L: turn left through about 135°.

m: metre. This is roughly a yard. All distances mentioned are rough, but near enough for purposes of following the route.

P: parking (off road). Free unless otherwise stated.

R: turn right through about 90°.

●: marks places where there is a choice of routes.

Hazards and problems

1. Boggy patches. Wettish areas have been avoided as far as possible. Even so, after a rainy spell, there may be some squelchy sections to cope with.

2. Snow and ice. These walks are mainly for the summer. Make sure you find out about winter hazards before going out in them.

3. Strong winds. Avoid aretes, like Striding Edge, or you may get blown off. It usually gets windier the higher you go.

4. Mist. Sometimes peaks are covered by a bank of low clouds. Do not walk up into this kind of mist. You will not see anything, and the chance of it lifting is small. If a belt of rain is forecast do not go up or you may run into a much wetter kind of mist. Even on a fine day, the tops may cloud over for a while near midday, but this seldom causes problems. With the above precautions, your chance of being caught in an unexpected mist is remote. And if it does happen, a retreat (if you have not yet reached the highest peak of the walk) is advised, unless otherwise stated. As a rule this is no problem, but occasionally *it is vital to have a compass, map and warm clothing.* So always take them.

5. Rough paths. For comfort and safety wear walking boots with thick soles and protection for the ankles. Scrambles (see glossary) in these walks are short and easy.

1:25,000 (2½ inches to the mile) OS Outdoor Leisure Maps

The four maps cover all walks except part of number 12. They are optional luxuries. One advantage is that they show walls and fences. But do not be misled by paths marked in green. Unless one of these is printed on top of a path marked in black, you may find no path at all. For example, the famous breast route from Sty Head to Great Gable is shown twice in green, and probably neither is accurately mapped.

Checklist

Essential items: rucksack (food, drink, first aid); boots, socks; clothes for wet, cold, windy weather; maps — Ordnance Survey and road; compass; money and keys.

Optional items: camera; binoculars; identification books; pencil and paper; sunglasses; whistle (in case of accident).

Weather forecast. Radio Carlisle on 206, 358, 397m or 95.6MHz; or telephone Windermere (096 62) 5151 after 8.15 a.m.

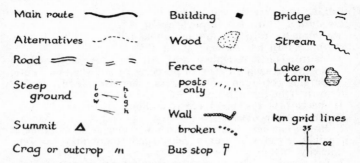

Main route	Building •	Bridge ≍
Alternatives ----''''''---	Wood	Stream
Road	Fence +++++	Lake or tarn
Steep ground	posts only ''''''''	
Summit △	Wall broken ••••••	km grid lines 35
Crag or outcrop ///	Bus stop	02

1. Fairfield Horseshoe *(17km, 10½mi, 3500ft)*

Map 90

Summary. A classic ridge walk where there is always a wall or steep ground on your L to guide you. The walk is long, but the paths mostly easy. You can save 2km (1¼mi) by getting a bus at Rydal.

Alternative: at 2 taking the path forking L after pines gets you on to the ridge sooner. Follow the wall. You will meet an easy rock step scramble.

Wordsworth lived at Rydal Mount for many years. In April enjoy the daffodils in Dora's Field by the church.

Parking (not free) by A591 just N of the junction with Kirkstone Road.

1 Climb Kirkstone Road (376047), which starts 150m N (i.e. towards Keswick) from Ambleside bus station. Soon turn L along lane. Soon take L fork. Ignore side turnings. **2** At lane end go on (do not fork R) 100m to bridge and over. Up winding stony (later grassy) track. Ignore path forking L just past some pines on your L. **3** Take R fork after passing through broken wall. On over wall with fold on your R. **4** Track bends L before a crag, gets smaller and soon reaches ridge wall. Turn R by ridge wall (on your L) over Low Pike and High Pike to Dove Crag. **5** On by wall which soon turns half L. **6** On up to Hart Crag, where wall stops. **7** Follow path and cairns (at first NW) to Fairfield. **8** Go S gently down the ridge past Great Rigg, Heron Pike and Nab Scar. (Steep ground on your L as far as Heron Pike.) **9** Soon there is a short steep section (with easier ground to L of rough path). Down past pines (on your L) and then house (on your R). **10** Here half R to road. Down road. **11** Soon after passing Rydal Mount, turn first L up track. Go half R at cross tracks. When another track is met go half L along it. **12** Go half L along road.

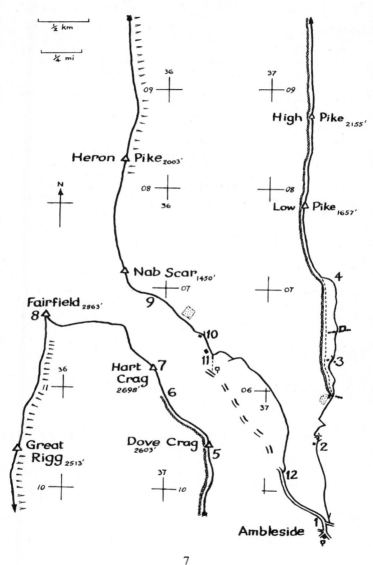

7

2. Red Screes *(13km, 8mi, 2400ft)*   Map 90

Summary. After a beautiful start, the far end of the valley is less interesting, but the fine summit views and the splendid easy ridge descent makes this a rewarding walk. If you have to retreat, try varying the return at 3: cross the bridge and stile at 3, go L 20m then R up near wall (on your R), over stile and L on meeting a path.

Peak baggers can go NW from summit to Middle Dodd and back, an extra 2km (1¼mi) and 450ft.

Parking (not free) by A591 just N of the junction with Kirkstone Road.

There are many attractive stone bridges in the district. Few of them are very old, though some stand on the sites of earlier ones. Some are packhorse bridges on ancient trading routes. Others simply serve to get sheep across between pastures separated by a stream. One of the best, High Sweden Bridge, is seen on this walk. A walk to this bridge and back on the other side of the beck is a fine walk in itself.

1 Climb Kirkstone Road (376047) which starts 150m N of Ambleside bus station **2** Turn L along Sweden Bridge Lane to its end. (Ignore road to Low Sweden Bridge on L and Ellerig Road on R.) On through gate. **3** 50m before bridge take path on up valley by wall on your R. **4** Over stream and past fold. **5** When in line with wall AB ignore path off L and make for col. **6** Here over stile and R up by wall, then half L to summit. **7** Sharp R (SW) down ridge. **8** When wall stops you, follow it R 100m then L between walls. **9** R down road. **10** Go half R along track between walls at first. On along path which later goes L through small gate by stream. On down track and then road.

3. Caudale Moor *(7km, 4¼mi, 2000ft)*

Map 90

Summary. This walk just qualifies for the book, Caudale Moor being 2502ft high. It starts with a rather vague path and tedious climb relieved only by pleasant views. It ends with an enjoyable, though somewhat steep, descent of a ridge towards Brothers Water. Sometimes wet ground near 7. Avoid in mist, as after passing Hartsop Dodd it is hard to find the path back. The only sure way would be to carry on by the wall at 7 all the way to the top of Kirkstone Pass — a long detour. This is the least good walk in the book.

Park in lay-by 400m S of Brotherswater Inn (403119). **1** From

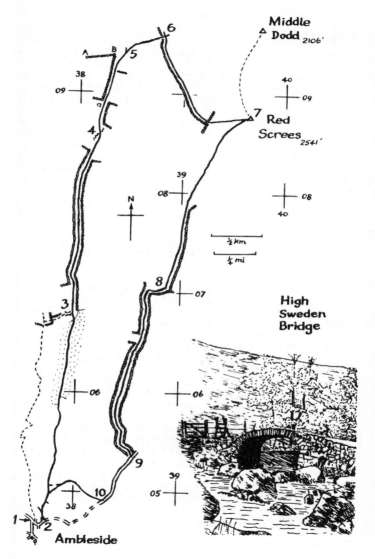

Middle Dodd 2106'

Red Screes 2541'

High Sweden Bridge

½ km
¼ mi

N

Ambleside

9

Caudale Bridge (402115) go N along road 100m towards lake and at gate turn R up path, soon by wall on your L. **2** As wall turns L path goes just R of wet area and bears L between small tree and outcrop. It then goes up on L of rushy stream and veers well to L of larger outcrop 100m higher up. It then turns R to this outcrop and becomes a clearer zig-zag path. Where a level path crosses yours, keep on up with a rushy groove on your R. Watch for next R turn beside rushes and ignore the faint path going on. Turn L with path 150m before outcrop ahead on skyline. **3** Near top path is vague, so go straight up past wooden post to Hartsop Dodd's cairn. **4** Go R along ridge path with wall on your L (or go along well to L of wall for views of valley). **5** Near wall corner on the flat top go L 100m to summit. **6** Turn back, staying on path (going W) with wall on your L. **7** When wall turns half L a second time, you turn R gently up to large cairn (no path). **8** Here go on (NW) soon on a path down ridge. **9** After passing mine on your R, turn R along wide path soon towards mine tip. Turn sharp L 100m before tips. **10** Path curves L and meets another wide path. Here go R down path, through wall gap, and down by stream on your R.

4. High Street from Haweswater *(11km, 6³⁄₄mi, 2600ft)*   Map 90

Summary. It is about 30 miles from Keswick to the start, 35 from Ambleside. Choose a good day and you will find this a superb excursion, starting with a splendid ridge and with views almost all the time — crags, lake and two delightful tarns. If necessary the walk can be shortened **at 7** by going L down a good path past Small Water (saves 2km, 1¼mi.) Very little of the route from High Street to Nan Bield Pass has a clear path, so take care (and a compass) if a mist appears, and get back via Small Water.

Park at SW end of Haweswater where road ends (470108). **1** Go on through gate just on R of footpath sign. Keep near wall (on your R). Turn R when wall goes R. **2** Over bridge and R by lakeside. Follow path as it rises to crest of ridge. **3** Here sharp L up ridge (wall on your R for a mile). **4** At end of ridge bear L to summit of High Street. **5** Go L (SE) down to top edge of crags. Along near edge (crags on your L) first down, then up to Mardale Ill Bell. **6** Turn two-thirds R (S) down ridge thus moving away from crags. After going about 400m bear L to rocky col (Nan Bield Pass). ●**7** Here on up to summit of Harter Fell. **8** Here go down (NE) by remains of old fence and cairns with steep ground on your L. Later these go two thirds R. **9** When crags on your L are passed, go L down grass to top of pass. **10** Here L down path.

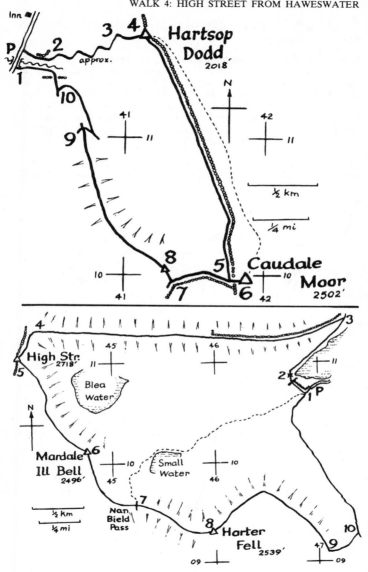

11

5. High Street from Hartsop *(14.5km, 9mi, 2700ft)*

Map 90

Summary. A fine introduction to the far eastern fells. Apart from a few short rough sections the route is easy on the feet and may seem shorter than it is. After climbing out of the valley you are on the tops and little effort is needed to reach the various summits. An obvious short cut is to stay on the direct path from 9 to 14, thus saving 3km (2mi) of walking. (Do this if mist comes down.) Peak baggers at 14 should go W through a wall gap to climb The Knott. The ground may be a bit wet at 4.

Leave A592 just N of Brothers Water and go E to Hartsop. **Park** at road end (410130). **1** Through gate at top of car park and half

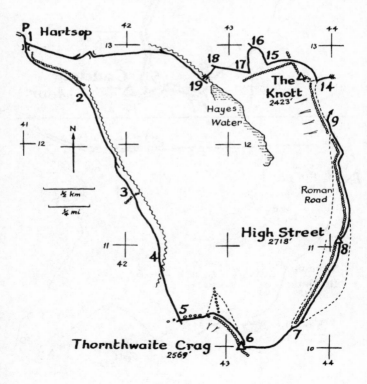

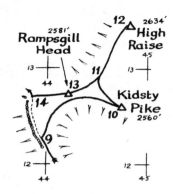

R over bridge. Then half L up to stile. Over it and L by wall (on your L). **2** On up valley by stream (on your L) at first. Then follow bare path gently climbing the valley side. (Ignore faint grass path that stays by stream.) **3** Through wall and along path passing just R of huge boulder. **4** On over short stretch of boggy ground (path vague; aim for cairn). Soon over stream and up steeper path to col. **5** Here go L by wall. First keep wall on your L. At scree it is easier to keep wall on your R (or easier still to go half L up grass and get back to wall when slope eases). **6** At 'beacon' go L (E) along path which bears L to distant wall. **7** On by wall (on your L) to High Street (or better go NE then N along crag tops to enjoy views). **8** On by wall. ●**9** After gap in wall, soon fork R along path to Kidsty Pike. **10** Turn back. Soon leave path and keep on a level course (NW) until a path is reached. **11** Follow this path R to the slight bump called High Raise. (Steep ground not far to your L all the way.) **12** Turn back. Take R fork, so keeping near steep ground (on your R). When path fades, go on gently up to the cairn at top of Rampsgill Head. **13** On down easy grass to clear path near wall. **14** R along path which bears L and goes through wall gap. Carry on with wall not far from your L until ground steepens at cairn. **15** Here turn R with path. **16** After short rough section go half L near big cairn along path. **17** Go R with path 20m before reaching wall. **18** Go half L down path to dam. **19** Over bridge and R down track.

6. St Sunday Crag *(12.5km, 7¾mi, 2400ft)*

Map 90

Summary. After a beautiful climb in Glenamara Park there is a fine high-level path with views of Ullswater before reaching the ridge. A short section of the descent to the tarn is on a narrow tilted path on the side of a steep hill. It can be avoided at 11 by

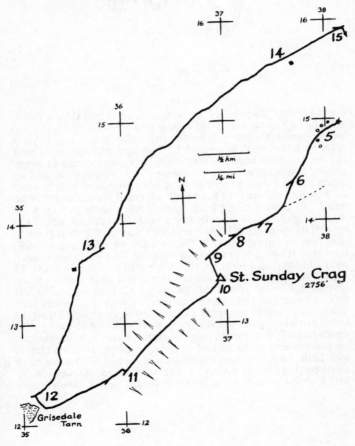

14

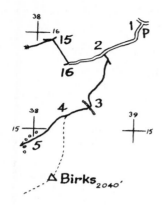

going down more than 50m, then turning L over grass at an easier gradient to rejoin the path further on. After enjoying the tarn, the return along the valley side is delightful, though you may object to the slight climb near the end. (If so, use the path R of Grisedale Beck by going on at 13.) Peak baggers can go half L at the cairn at 4 to climb Birks.

Park just up side road at Grisedale Bridge (390161) between Glenridding and Patterdale, or by the old school on the main road ¼mi E of this. **1** Up side road to signpost by gate. **2** Here L along track up field. After 100m go half R over stile and up path among trees. **3** Cross wall at stile. **4** Keep on when path levels and becomes grassy. **5** Path climbs near broken wall (on your R) for 100m, then crosses wall. **6** When path changes from grass to bare earth watch for fork. Go one third L here. **7** Ignore path forking L where ground starts to steepen. **8** At top of rise take L fork, thus bearing slightly away from edge. **9** When Grisedale Tarn and path below it are seen, go half L to rocky summit. **10** Go half R along ridge to col. **11** Here go R down grass 50m (scree on your L) then L up clear path. It soon levels, then drops. Soon take R fork down. **12** When path fades go two thirds R over grass to track just R of tarn. R down track. **13** After lodge go L over bridge. **14** On past farm. **15** At cross path go R through gate, down field and on along track to road. **16** Here L along road.

7. Helvellyn from Ullswater *(13km, 8mi, 3100ft)*

Map 90

Summary. An excellent excursion. Leaving out Catstycam saves you 1km (¾mi) and 300ft of climb. Excitement mounts after reaching the wall gap. Red Tarn cradled in the crags of Helvellyn is enjoyed from various angles. The traverse of Striding Edge is magnificent. It involves one easy scramble up rocks near its start. Cautious individuals may prefer to sneak round the base of the rocks to the right of the path.

There is limited parking near Grisedale Bridge in the minor road, and more (¼mi E of this) in the main road at the old school.

Alternative start. Park (at a price) in Glenridding (387169). **A** Go W along lane on the other side of river from car park. **B** Fork L up rough track. **C** After houses go L up path. On up zigzags past an attractive pool and down to junction of tracks. **3** Here go one third R up the 'gently climbing path'. **4 to 8** as main route. **9** At gate 200m before pool keep on (soon by wood on your R) to reach path you came up. Go L down it.

1 Start at Grisedale Bridge (390161) between Glenridding and Patterdale. Go (SW) along the minor road. **2** Go R at its end, down to bridge and up to wall. **3** Here go two thirds L up path. Follow the gently climbing path. **4** At gap in wall use nearly level path to pass just R of tarn. **5** Here climb to clear path and L along it. **6** At ridge go sharp R to Catstycam and back. Then on up rocky ridge to Helvellyn. **7** On with crags on your L, then down fairly steep rough ground to the start of Striding Edge. On along top of ridge back to gap in wall. **8** This time keep on by wall (kept on your R) along the ridge and later down by wall. ● **9** At gate 200m before pool in trees, go two thirds R (SE) down

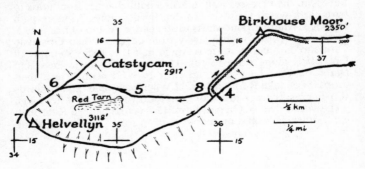

16

Striding Edge.

grass towards R hand end of the L of two small pinewoods. **10** Here, R along track, then L to road.

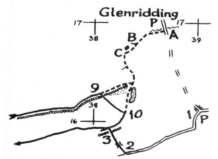

Striding Edge. This magnificent arete is seen from walks 8 and 9 and traversed in walk 7. After a rough descent from Helvellyn, the exhilarating walk along the edge begins, with Red Tarn below on the left. It is a very popular route. The sides are far from precipitous, and people have been known to make their way laboriously down a side rather than stay on top. Even so, take care in strong winds; being blown over the edge would be at least very unpleasant and probably disastrous. But in normal weather relax and enjoy it.

8. Helvellyn from Wythburn *(12km, 7½mi, 2700ft)*

Map 90

Summary. This walk includes a visit to Grisedale Tarn, then the most spectacular section of the Helvellyn ridge, and views of Thirlmere on the way down. Paths are very good, except for two rough sections — one above the tarn, the other well down on the descent. If mist appears at Dollywaggon Pike, carry on along the clear wide path and go sharp L (at 12) down clear path at col. The large cairn at the top of Dunmail Raise (328117) is said to commemorate Dunmail, the last king of Cumbria ('Raise' is the Viking word for cairn.)

Park at Wythburn (324137) on the A591, 14km (8mi) S from Keswick. **1** Up path by car park in wood. **2** R along cross track. **3** On out of wood. **4** Where wall on your R turns R, cross bridge, then go half L to step-stile and stile on to road. **5** L along road 100m, then L over step-stile. Follow the path by Raise Beck (on your L). **6** If it becomes wet and vague look for a better parallel path a few metres to R. **7** When ground levels pass L of tarn to join steep zigzag path. **8** Up this path. **9** When gradient eases go half R off path to summit of Dollywaggon Pike. **10** Go NW along top of crags. When path is rejoined it can be used, but it is better

On the ridge south of Helvellyn.

18

to stay on the ridge with steep ground on your R most of the way. **11** At Helvellyn summit (just past stone shelter) turn back to col. **12** Here fork R along clear track that soon descends.

19

9. Helvellyn from Thirlspot *(13km, 8mi, 3200ft)*

Map 90

Summary. Not the best ascent of Helvellyn, as a few sections cross somewhat dreary moorland and there are several boggy patches. It is included for the ascent of Whiteside and Raise, and for the splendid waterfalls at 5. If you are feeling energetic go S from Helvellyn to Nethermost Pike and back for exciting views.

Park at Stanah (318189) 8km (5mi) from Keswick on the A591. **1** Go S along road (away from Keswick). **2** Just past King's Head Inn go L up farm track between buildings. Over bridge and up field to gate at second bridge. **3** Over bridge and half L to wooden gate. Through it and along by wall on your L. **4** After crossing stream, path bears gently away from wall. Ignore path on R (marked by white stones) 20m after stream. Soon on over two streams 10m apart. 100m after these, ignore path going half R. When ravine is seen 150m ahead take the smaller nearly level path, not the one forking half R. **5** Turn R up past two waterfalls. **6** When third fall is seen 150m ahead leave path. Go R over grass keeping level or gently climbing. Make for ruin when it is seen. **7** Turn up path by ruin. Path soon bears R (ignore thin path forking L). It heads for Brown Crag and then Whiteside. **8** If boggy go round to L. **9** Soon path levels, so contouring round Whiteside. **10** Path bears L and runs by stream. Where it fades follow cairns to ridge. **11** R along ridge to summit and back. **12** Then on to top of Whiteside. **13** Go two thirds R down to col and up (follow cairns) to Raise. **14** Follow cairns half L down other side. When stony area ends go on 100m to clear grass path. Near a boggy patch follow strip of greener shorter grass that goes slightly R and soon reaches Sticks Pass. **15** L along clear path. **16** At wall go R over bridge and at once L through gate. Down path to bridge. Over stile here, down path to wall stile. Down to main road.

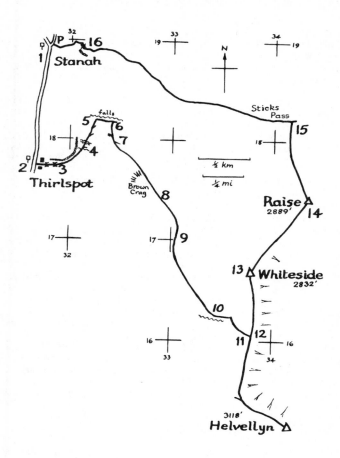

10. The Clough Head Ridge *(15.5km, 9¾mi, 2900ft)*

Map 90

Summary. A long walk, but the paths are easy. The ridge is on delightful short turf once 7 is passed. If you do not fancy the scree at 2 and 4 stay on the Old Coach Road: at two gates go through the R (wooden) one; cross mine road; at gate go on keeping just R of fence; at highest point (or before) go R up pathless grass to 6 (passing to R of White Pike). This adds 1½km (1mi). The long return along St John in the Vale is very pleasant and at places runs by the beck.

A variation is to start at Dale Bottom (295217) and walk over the little used road to the start (lay-by 200m NW of junction). At Stanah a bus may be taken to get back. This shortens the walk by about 1km (¾mi).

Not recommended if there is a chance of mist as the ridge twists and turns, mostly without paths.

Park near start of Old Coach Road (316231) 2km (1¼mi) S of Threlkeld. **1** Go up this 'road' (a rough track signposted 'Matterdale'). **2** Soon there is a wall on your R. When it turns back, go half R up scree path between mine tips, then cross two mine roads. **3** On up steep grass near quarry edge on your L. Over stile and on up clear sunken path. Later it veers L, then R, at cairns. **4** Path gets vague at a slight col where there is a rock (1m high) 10m L of path. Keep on gently up to two or three cairns marking start of path winding up scree and bearing R. (Ignore obvious scree-less path going off R before these cairns are reached.) Soon a firm path climbs to ridge. **5** Here turn sharp L to top of Clough Head. **6** Here turn sharp R to go almost S towards Calfhow Pike, a small knob of rock. **7** Here turn half L, soon climbing a broad ridge to Great Dodd. **8** Here go sharp R (SW) down and along an almost level ridge to Watson's Dodd. **9** Here turn L (SE) with the ridge to climb Stybarrow Dodd. **10** Here go R down ridge (no path). **11** Pick up clear path lower down. **12** At wall go R over bridge and at once L through gate. Down path to bridge. Over stile here, down path to wall stile. Down to road. **13** Go half R along main road. **14** Just after bridge go R up a gently rising path. After 50m ignore the steeply rising path forking L. The path climbs, then drops and bears L away from river, with wall on your R. **15** Near house climb to pass just L of it and back down to river path, soon on raised bank. **16** On past bridge (now below bank on your R), and on along line of trees (fence on your R). **17** Then one third L over field to post by bridge. On to stile. **18** On along grass track to stile. On by stream, then river. **19** R at road and R again to start.

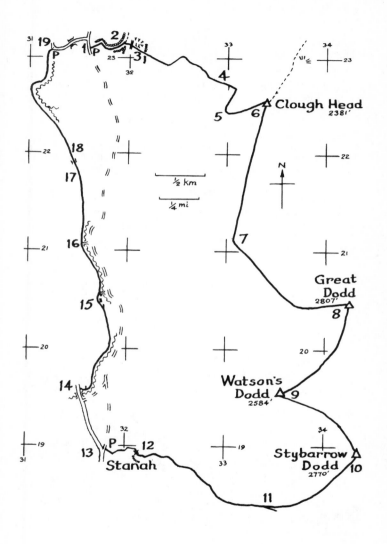

23

11. Blencathra *(11km, 7mi, 2600ft)* Map 90

Summary. Blencathra is an isolated mountain with magnificent ridges on its south side, one of which is used for the ascent. Its tarn will be seen in impressive surroundings below the rocks of Sharp Edge. To make an easy day's walk the splendid summit ridge is traversed twice. Fine views are also seen on Bannerdale Crags, before descending. To omit these crags go R at 10 using path on L or R of stream.

The adventurous could keep on by wall at 2 until they reach the path going up the next ridge. It has one tricky section where a rock is traversed with an uncomfortably long and steep drop below. Another variation at 5 is to go down to the tarn, pass to its R, and bear L up the grassy ridge behind it, then along the narrow Sharp Edge, ending with a steep scramble up rock, not for the nervous. At 10 Bowscale Fell could be visited by going L(N) but it deserves a separate expedition.

Escape route at 5: go on down to stream just R of tarn. Go R down path that starts on far side of stream.

Park in lay-by near start of walk.

The walk starts (at 340267) E of Threlkeld on A66 300m SW of inn at Scales. **1** Go up between two houses, through gate and L along by wall. **2** At stream scramble down and up rocks to cross it. Soon, when path starts to descend, turn R up grassy path in bracken. **3** Follow path on when bracken ends (or bear L to

Blencathra from the Old Coach Road.

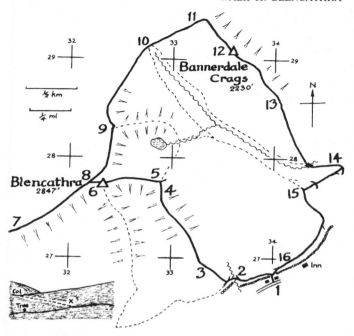

reach ridge earlier). **4** Near top of ridge keep just R of scree shoot. At cairn scree bends L, but you keep on along clear path to grassy top. ● **5** Here L to summit of Blencathra. **6** On by steep ground (on your L) until ground ahead drops more steeply. **7** Turn back towards summit. **8** When near summit bear L across 'saddle' towards second (lower) summit. You pass small tarn, cairn, cross of white stones and two more cairns. **9** 20m after this turn L down path. When path fades, bear R to keep by steep ground (on your R) and reach col. ● **10** Keep on gently up, then down, to edge of crags. **11** Here R along edge to summit of Bannerdale Crags. **12** On down near edge. **13** When ground ahead steepens, aim for R end of clear path (marked X on drawing). When bridge is seen, go down and cross it. Go gently up to col. **14** Here turn R (gently up) soon joining clear path along this low ridge that connects Souther Fell with Blencathra. When another path is met go on 200m (no path) to reach main path. **15** Go L along this, passing several rocky outcrops. Follow clear bare stony path. Later it keeps well above the wall. **16** Fork L down to gate near start.

12. Skiddaw from the north *(13km, 8mi, 2800ft)*

Map 89 or 90

Summary. The best way to 'do' Skiddaw, starting with an excellent ridge. The only hard bit is the final climb to Skiddaw. If mist comes down on this final climb it is probably better to keep going to the top. (To visit Skiddaw Little Man, turn R down clear path on reaching the final ridge to the summit. Leave path near fence and go on to Little Man with fence on your L. Return the same way. This adds 2km (1½mi) to the walk. Or go on by the fence to rejoin the clear path for a direct return to Keswick.) The descent is easy. The fence may be left at Bakestall to add interest by using a path along the top of the crags. Enjoy Dash Falls seen on the final road section.

The ridge can also be reached by a path starting S of Ravenstone Hotel (235297).

At High Side on the A591 8km (5mi) N of Keswick a minor road forks R. **Park** 400m beyond fork at 237310 on minor road. **1** Just past lay-by go half R up track. Go R at line of trees (no path).

Skiddaw from Derwentwater.

26

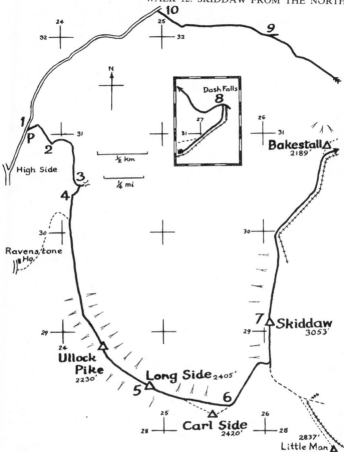

2 100m past trees turn L along track to stile. On along track, which soon bears R. **3** 50m before footbridge and fold go up grass passing by scree and rocks on your R (vague paths). **4** When on ridge top go half L along ridge path to Ullock Pike and Long Side. **5** On to the col below the vast slaty side of Skiddaw. (The path passes L of Carl Side, which can be visited if you wish.) **6** At col go NE up slaty path to Skiddaw. **7** Go on (N) and soon go half R down by fence (on your R) to the track near Dash Falls. **8** L along this. **9** On at junction. **10** L at minor road.

27

13. High Spy to Catbells *(14.5km, 9¼mi, 2400ft)*

Map 89 or 90

Summary. The complete traverse of an excellent ridge, with fine views of Newlands Valley and Derwentwater, is combined with a lower path which is still high enough for good views, yet adorned with a variety of trees. Part of this is a permissive path, starting at 3. Without this, the road would have to be walked to Grange. If a bus is taken to Grange, cross bridge and soon go L along lane to 6. (Use road to get back from 3.)

Although the highest peak (High Spy) is only 2143 feet, this is a real mountain walk, though not too tiring to the feet. There is some easy scrambling on the descent of Catbells. A much shorter version is to fork R at 2 and later go sharp R up clear path to col (rather steep and rough higher up). Here R to Catbells etc (5km, 3¼mi).

If mist comes down at 12 it is better to carry on (along the clear ridge path) unless you are sure you can find your way back to 10.

Park in or near old quarry by road (249198) above Brandlehow on W side of Derwentwater. **1** Go L (S) along path starting at L edge of quarry. It runs parallel to road. **2** On by wall (on your L) near pines. **3** At road go up by two posts near house to stile. Into pines and out, L to wall, then R along by wall or fence on your L. **4** Skirt damp area, cross stream and on along clear dry path by fence. **5** Turn L at stile (wood and wall on your L). Soon R along by wall (on your L). **6** Soon after passing Hollows fork R (at first between walls). **7** On by river for 100m, then on up wide track (signed 'Seatoller') which soon bears R. **8** At top of rise, stay on main track that soon bears R away from wall. **9** On up by stream (on your L). After second bridge, when ground gets too rough, go up other side of stream for a bit then return (path now indistinct). **10** Up middle of tongue (no path; easy but tedious grass). **11** As ground levels go R along clear path, soon crossing stream and some stepping stones. Soon, at cairn, go half L off path, making for 'fold' (two isolated bits of wall). Pass just L of fold, up grass slope. **12** Skirt boggy ground (keeping it on your L), soon reaching clear cairned ridge path leading you to High Spy. **13** On past Blea Crag keeping by steep ground on your L to the slight rise to Maiden Moor. **14** On down ridge to col and up to Catbells. **15** On down ridge. **16** Down steep rocky section after long flattish stretch. Here bear half R down grass (ignore path forking R), then R down easy zigzags. **17** When road at end of ridge is seen 100m away, turn R down more zigzags to track just above road. Go R along track.

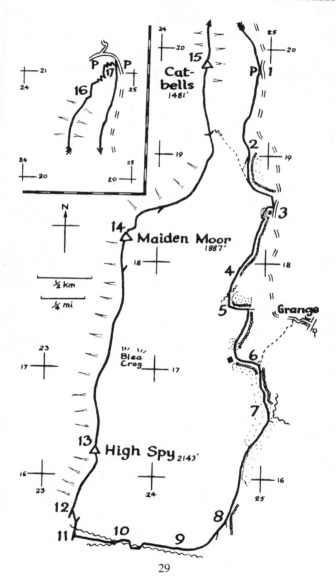

Cat-
bells
1481'

Maiden Moor
1887'

Grange

Blea
Crag

High Spy 2143'

N

½ km

¼ mi

29

14. Robinson to Dale Head *(12.5km, 7¾mi, 2600ft)*

Map 89 or 90

Summary. A fine walk, not quite reaching 2500ft, well worth repeating with one of the variations suggested here. Soon you are on a splendid ridge and stay on ridges until the final descent. Bear in mind there is a scramble at 4 on firm rock with plenty of foot and hand holds. If you do not enjoy scrambles, avoid Robinson altogether, as follows. Fork L at church and soon fork L again. Pass farm, go through gate and R up path. At ridge go L up clear path to Hindscarth, on to fence and L to Dale Head etc (1.5km, 1mi shorter).

Also near 10 some may not like the short scree crossing. If so, do not go sharp L at second cairn, but go down to next cairn and sharp L along a firm path that works across steep ground. If this does not appeal, do not go sharp L but keep on down, later over a stream and L down good path that rejoins the main walk near 13.

At 8, Hindscarth can be visited by going L along the broad ridge. Turn back or keep on along the narrowing ridge for a delightful descent. (At fence go R to stony track, L along track, soon through gate and on past farm. This return shortens walk to 10.5km, 6½mi.)

Park near bridge (232193) just SW of Little Town in Newlands Valley (W of Derwentwater). **1** Go W over bridge and at once L. Soon fork R by church. **2** Pass buildings and on through two gates. Then go R by wall (on your R) for 20m. Then fork L up path to ridge top. **3** Go half L along ridge. **4** Scramble up rocks (perhaps easier on the R). **5** At large cairn at top of rise follow cairns on to Robinson. **6** Go half L (S) on cairned path to fence. **7** Go half L by fence down, then up. **8** At top go half R by fence to Dale Head. **9** On down by steep edge (on your L) to cairn where path turns half R. **10** 15m past this cairn turn sharp L at second cairn and go gently down small grass path. This crosses scree and becomes clearer and well cairned as it descends rock-strewn slopes. **11** On past mine ruin, now on grass path. Watch for the sharp R turn (zigzag) that eases the slope. **12** After passing ravine, the grass path goes on towards the R of patch of rushes near stream. **13** When path fades, cross side stream. Cross main stream near rush patch. Go L along bank 50m. On along track. **14** Go L by wall to bridge and over. Follow wall round to R. Through gate and on past farm.

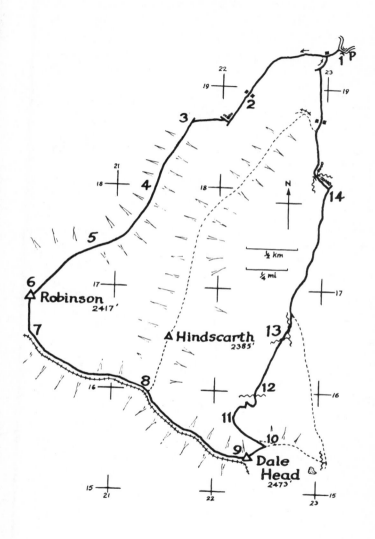

31

15. Causey Pike to Eel Crag *(14km, 8¾mi, 3000ft)*

Map 89 or 90

Summary. A splendid ridge up to Eel Crag, with an easy scramble on Causey Pike. The return is easy with good views of Skiddaw.

Escape route: At col between Causey Pike and Scar Crags go half R (NW) down grass to reach path at B. (Keep L of boggy area.) R down path with stream on R.

Short cut. This adds 700ft of climb, but saves 2.5km (1½mi). Follow 1 to 9 then **10** At cairn on bend in track (opposite mine sheds) go up grass path. On up grass when path fades. **A** Go L along path you meet, soon with stream on R.

Start at bridge (232212) on Newlands Pass near Stair 2.5km (1½mi) S of Braithwaite. **Park** here or N of bridge. **1** At S end of bridge go half R up path. Make for path seen ahead rising steeply up Rowling End. Cross some level paths. (Those who prefer an easier start can fork R along path seen gently rising up the side of Rowling End.) **2** On along ridge. **3** On when alternative path reaches ridge. **4** At final rocky dome of Causey Pike either scramble straight up firm rock, or go 10m L along

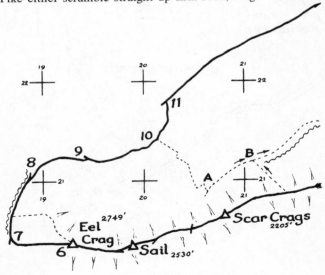

level path and then scramble sharp R up firm rock. Soon you come to a gulley slanting up to the L (not obvious until reached). Here go L 5m and scramble up firm rock. **5** On along ridge to Scar Crags, Sail and triangulation column on Eel Crag (Crag Hill). **6** Go W down grass towards Grasmoor, the large mountain ahead. (Or go NW along ridge and then down steeper grass. Do not go too far or you get to scree.) **7** R along path, soon with stream on its L. **8** Ignore path going down by rocky stream. Take main path which bears R and soon descends (ENE) towards distant mine road along valley. Follow this cairned winding path. **9** Go half R along track. • **10** Ignore grass path on R. **11** Over stream. Up to mine road. R along it. **12** As road bears L keep on along path through gorse. **13** Go R down road. **14** R over bridge and soon L along rough road. At junction go half R up road. **15** Where road bends L go on up drive. **16** On past farm up small field to open fell. Here go half L along path not far from fence on the L. **17** On along road.

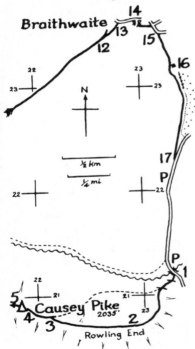

33

16. Whiteside to Grisedale Pike *(13.5km, 8½mi, 2400ft)*

Map 89

Summary. An excellent long ridge, made into a circular walk by using a delightful high level lane and plantations. If you want to leave the lane until last and start climbing right away, it is possible to park near 4 in the gated lane (169242). (Or the whole walk can be reversed, but only if you are sure you know which ridge of Whiteside to descend.) If mist appears after 11 it is best to keep going to 14. There you may prefer to follow the old wall down NE to the road.

The best ascent of Grisedale Pike starts at a car park (227237) after the Whinlatter Pass road bends R after leaving Braithwaite. Simply go NW up steps and soon bear L up the wide path (100m before forest) all the way up the splendid ridge.

Park by plantation entrance (192245) opposite the unwooded area of N of Whinlatter Pass 1.5km (1mi) W of top of pass. **1** Go down road. **2** At road signpost fork L along lane. **3** Fork L. Later through gate marked 'High Swinside Farm'. **4** 100m before next gate on road, go one third L along path, soon near wall (on your R). At small stream take R fork (see drawing). **5** 80m before larger stream fork L down to it. When 10m from this stream turn R and cross it. **6** After 5m fork L up slight path which bears L. At several forks always fork L up, thus passing to the R of the nearby grassy hillock. **7** Soon path has a groove or ditch on its R

Hopehill Head from Grisedale Pike.

34

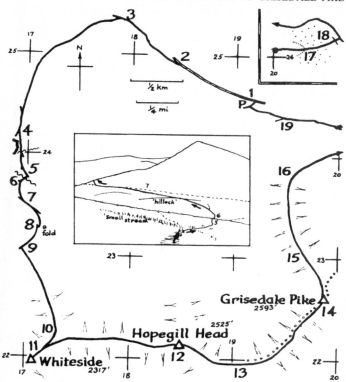

and is joined by another path coming from R. 100m later fork half R up path which also soon has a groove on its R. It bears R keeping to R of patches of rushes. **8** At a ruined fold go up 20m to join clear path leading L to col. **9** Here go L (SE) up ridge (no path). **10** When near top bear R to summit of Whiteside. **11** Turn back (NE) along main ridge path with steep ground on your R to pyramid top of Hopegill Head. **12** Go one third R down to col by crags on your L. **13** Follow old wall on up to Grisedale Pike summit. (*You go over one minor summit on the way.*) **14** Here turn L (NW) down broad ridge without a path. (*Not* the ridge with old stone wall going NE). **15** On along path. **16** At end of level section follow path half R down to trees. **17** On down fire break. On over grass track down to forest track. **18** L along this track, soon parallel to road. **19** Fork R. Soon turn R to road.

35

17. Grasmoor to Whiteless Pike *(9.5km, 6mi, 2700ft)*

Map 89

Summary. A fine walk with views all the way. From Grasmoor it is worth going W down to Grasmoor End for an aerial view of Crummock Water. When returning keep near steep ground on your L for dramatic views including Dove Crags. Peak baggers could go on (E) to Eel Crag before 'doing' Wanlope. In mist go direct from 5 to 7 to keep on a path.

An alternative gentler and more sheltered route starts at Lanthwaite Green (158207). It is 3km (2mi) longer. **A** Take path E over grass towards heathery cone (Whin Ben). **B** Over bridge, go L 100m then R up path. At wide grass path go R along it. Path goes up valley by stream on your R (A few easy scrambles on firm rock). **C** Near col bear R with path. Soon after path comes in from L cross stream and climb (no path) with steep ground on your R to Grasmoor. Then follow 4 to 12.

To avoid road return from Rannerdale Common, use path parallel to road 100m from it. It climbs to base of scree to skirt bogs and goes on faintly through bracken. Not too easy to follow here, but it reaches road near car park if you are lucky.

Park at Rannerdale Common (163194) about 3 km (2mi) NW of Buttermere village. **1** Start up the path on L of stream. (It is

A pocket of snow on Grasmoor.

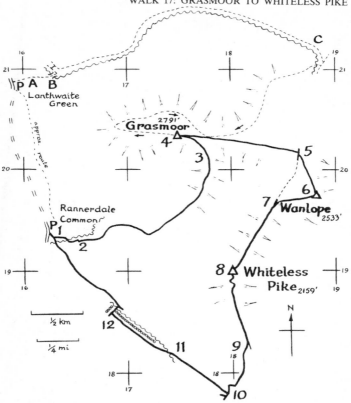

mostly 10m or so away from stream). Cross stream (near tree) and up path on R of stream. **2** Soon, at a rocky section, the path moves 10m further away from stream. Soon path keeps on where stream bears L. Follow path which winds up to the ridge and then go L up it. **3** At ridge top bear L to summit. **4** Turn round and go ESE down cairned path to col. **5** Here turn R along path and at once fork half L along fading path to the slight rise (Wanlope). **6** Here turn R (no path) to rejoin the one you left. **7** Go half L along this path, soon on narrow ridge to Whiteless Pike. **8** On down path. **9** After steep section follow path as it bears R along side of broad ridge. **10** Sharp R down path in valley. **11** Over stream, soon with wall or fence on your R. **12** At wall go R over stile and bridge, then L on grass track.

18. The High Stile Ridge *(13km, 8mi, 2600ft)*

Map 89

Summary. A very fine ridge with everything you could expect: lakes, a tarn, plenty of crags, a mass of heather and a waterfall. One or two boggy patches may be met, and some walkers may find the final descent to Scale Force tedious. The usual route reaches the ridge by the Scarth Gap path, but the final climb to High Crag is very steep on scree. Our version gives you an extra mile on the ridge and avoids scree.

There is some free parking at Buttermere, including space at the bottom of the road to Newlands Pass and 300m along road towards Crummock Water.

1 At Buttermere (174170) go along track (SW) past Fish Hotel (on your R). **2** At gates go half R along the L of two tracks. **3** At next gate go half R to bridge and over it. Bear L to go over small bridge and soon through gate. **4** Here go sharp R for 10m then sharp L up path to track. Cross this and go on up rocky path in wood. **5** After wood the path bears R. Where the path is rough and wide follow cairns along its L edge. **6** Near wall and trees fork R along smaller path to stream. Go up by stream, kept on your R. **7** 100m after wall starts, turn L (SSE, no path) over gently rising ground to highest point on old wall 250m away. **8** Here aim just R of the clear small horizontal strip of rock A shown in the drawing. (It has a long strip of scree B just on its L.) Near A go up grass between two scree patches, C, D (the L one is quite small) and bear slightly L to go up beside small rock outcrops on your L. Soon you are between scree B and rock outcrops. When a grassy, less steep area is reached make for large cairn F on skyline. **9** Follow faint path just R of cairn F. It goes half R (SW) along ridge passing slightly L of rocky top with iron post on its top. Follow cairns to reach fence posts. **10** Follow these L to High Crag and back. **11** Leave posts to visit summit of High Stile and for view. Then follow posts NW along ridge. **12** At top of rise go half R to Red Pike. **13** Go L (NW) down ridge. (Rough at first. To avoid this go sharp L (SW) from summit, keeping L of stony ground; at fence go R along it; get back to ridge when clear of stony area). **14** Watch for and take path (not too clear at start) going L to reach two cairns on rocks after 150m. Here follow cairned path (NW) to stream. (One boggy patch.) **15** Bear R keeping stream on your L. **16** After steep descent admire Scale Force (waterfall). Beside bridge go half R up path to wall and on along level path. Soon one boggy patch. **17** At next bog go L down a line of stones and cairns. **18** Go R at last cairn (faint path, soon clear). **19** Soon after path runs along bottom edge of wood go L over bridge then R along track. L at gate.

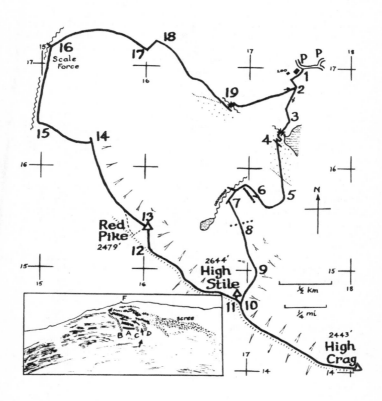

19. The Gables from Honister *(11.5km, 7mi, 2900ft)*

Map 89 or 90

Summary. Grey Knotts has a fine rocky top. Then it is easy going to Green Gable, a top with a fine view of Gable Crag. Great Gable is rough, but this is the easiest way of climbing it. The summit is well worth exploring in the SW direction for views of Wasdale and crags. The descent from Great Gable is rough, steep and tedious. It can be avoided as follows in clear weather. Go NE down the more grassy, less stony ground towards distant fields. Soon bear slightly R to dodge more stones. The path you came up should be 70m to your L. Work back towards this path, so that you join it where your ground gets steeper and boulder-strewn. Here you start down the firm rock. Retrace steps to 7, then carry on along path to 15 etc. Views towards Buttermere make the return very satisfying.

Leaving out Kirk Fell shortens the walk to 8½km, 5¼mi, 2200ft. Those who do not like retracing steps on the visit to Kirk Fell can make a different start from the col (12): go NW along a good gently descending path that finally rises to the top of Black Sail Pass. Here turn L to follow fence posts past a steep scramble to the summit and on to 12.

1 From car park at top of Honister Pass (226136) go towards mine buildings to reach fence. Here L by fence, then half R to start climb up by fence on your R. **2** Ignore stile at end of the first steepish section. **3** Where fence bears L keep on over stile and up cairned path. **4** Go half R beside old fence posts for 20m, then L to one or more of the rocky tops. **5** Go back to them. Follow them (SW) along broad ridge past small tarns. **6** At Brandreth follow posts half L down to cairned path. **7** Go half L along this path, passing to L of tarns. **8** Up path to Green Gable. (After the rocky rise you can avoid the stony path by walking on grass 20m to R.) **9** On down to col (using grassy strips on L to avoid most of the loose stones). **10** On and up. After easy rock scramble and stony path at easier gradient, bear L over to summit of Great Gable. **11** Follow cairns sharp R, NW towards a rough path on Kirk Fell. (The memorial tablet faces N towards the path you came up.) Take care you do not follow cairns NNW towards a distant lake (Crummock Water). Soon a rough path takes you down to col. To visit Kirk Fell summit follow fence posts past a minor summit and a tarn. Retrace your steps. **12** Near fence posts go E gently down path which soon contours round on the side of the Gables keeping nearly level. **13** Pass by fold at bend in path. **14** After gentle rise and 150m before some small rock outcrops fork R along path. **15** At top of slight rise fork one third R on small level path (NE) to fence posts. On 30m, then L down clear cairned path. **16** 100m before drum house keep on to reach it near its L end. **17** R along old tramway. **18** R along mine road, passing just L of buildings.

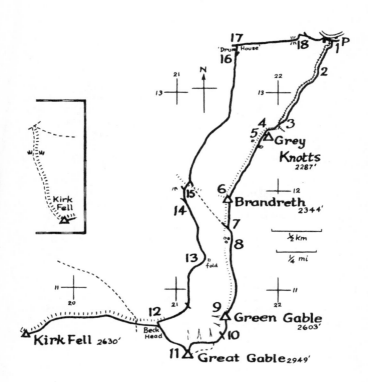

41

20. Glaramara *(13.5km, 8½mi, 2700ft)*

Map 89 or 90

Summary. An easy ascent by an attractive rocky stream at first. Boggy patches higher up are well supplied with stepping stones but the walk should be avoided in a rainy season. After the fine rocky summit of Glaramara there is a splendid ridge with several small but beautiful tarns to add to the views. If you have spare energy keep on at 9 to visit Sprinkling Tarn. The return follows Grains Gill. It is rather steep and rough at first.

The walk can also be reached from the Borrowdale road at Mountain View 500m E of Seatoller.

Start at Seathwaite (236123), Borrowdale, S of Keswick. **1** Where road ends park and go on past farm. Soon at signpost 'Borrowdale via Thornythwaite' go sharp L through gate and along path by wall on your L. **2** Do not go through gate near farm among pines, but bear R by wall and on along farm track. **3** When track bends L by stream, go over stile and up grassy track. This bears R and becomes stony. **4** Through gate and on up path by stream. Soon after fold, fork R up clear rough path. (Where path is red and seems to stop at rocks, keep on over these rocks.) Follow cairned path to rocks just below summit. **5** Up rock step and half R to Glaramara (or avoid this scramble by bearing round just to R of steep rocks). **6** On (SW) down towards second summit and along cairned path passing to L of this summit. **7** After several ups and downs you will know you have just passed Allen Crags when you see two wide paths ahead below you and Sprinkling Tarn on the R. Go on down, then bear R down easy scree to cairn at T junction on red path. **8** Here R (NW) down red path soon by ravine on your R. **9** When clear path is seen diagonally rising on opposite bank, cross to this path which goes down by ravine (now on your L). **10** Just past bottom of ravine it is more pleasant to cross stream to a red path that goes down L of stream. Cross back soon where path on R of stream bends R. **11** R over second bridge.

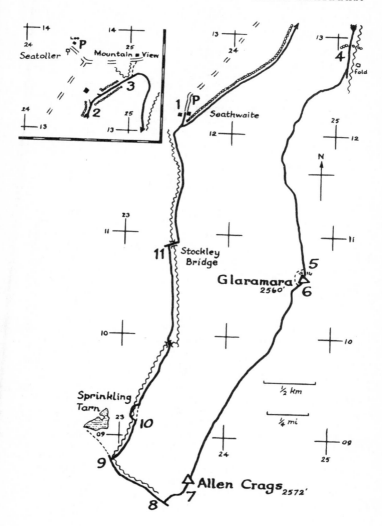

Seatoller
Mountain View
Seathwaite
Stockley Bridge
Glaramara 2560'
Sprinkling Tarn
Allen Crags 2572'

½ km
¼ mi

N

43

21. Great End and Esk Pike *(14.5km, 9mi, 3000ft)*

Map 89 or 90

Summary. A splendid and rugged walk. If Esk Pike is not visited you save 1.5km (1mi). If mist comes down at 9 or 10 turn back; if it comes at 11 do not go to Great End, but go on to reach clear track and follow it L down to the path junction 14. It is well worth exploring the NE edge of Great End's flat top for impressive views down several gullies.

There is another start on the other side of the stream, reached by a track through a farm building. It involves scrambling on an 'edgy' path and some wettish ground but gives fine views of the waterfall and saves you repeating the route N of Stockley Bridge. If mists shroud the tops a fine walk can still be enjoyed by keeping on up at 7 to pass Sprinkling Tarn and rejoining the route by going L at the ravine (9km, 5½mi).

1 At the road end at Seathwaite (235122), S of Keswick, park and go on through farm to Stockley Bridge. 2 Go R over bridge and on up winding path, later past pines on your R. 3 At top of pines path bears L, then R. Follow cairns. 4 When bridge is seen, reach it, keeping close to stream (on your R). Over bridge and L by stream. 5 On past tarn to stretcher box. 6 Here go L on line of stones (over boggy ground). 7 After a slight descent go R down small cairned path which skirts scree. 8 Scramble up rock step. (To avoid this, leave path about 100m before it and cross grass aiming to reach Skew Gill 100m to R of rock step. Cross here and turn L up grass to top of rock step.) Keep on up path. 9 Later it becomes nearly level and crosses two small streams. ● Here leave path and go up rough grass and scattered rocks (as shown in first drawing) to pass L of large rounded rock A. Bear R as slope eases to reach small tarn. Pass to R of tarn. 10 Just beyond rock (B in second drawing) near end of tarn go L up grassy strip and R mainly on grass along the base of scree area C. Later bear L to col D. (You can try the obvious route along grass at top of scree. It ends with short unpleasant bits of steep scree.) 11 Here go L along cairned path to Great End NW summit. 12 Go sharp R(SE) to the other summit. 13 Go R (SW then S) back to col and sharp L down rough path. 14 At path junction go half R up small path to Esk Pike and back. If you leave out this peak, turn L at this junction. If not, on return to junction, turn half R. 15 Soon you join large path by red ravine. 16 When clear path is seen diagonally rising on opposite bank, cross to this path which goes down by ravine (now on your L). 17 Just past bottom of ravine it is more pleasant to cross stream to a red path that goes down L of stream. Cross back soon where path on R of stream bends R. 18 R over second bridge.

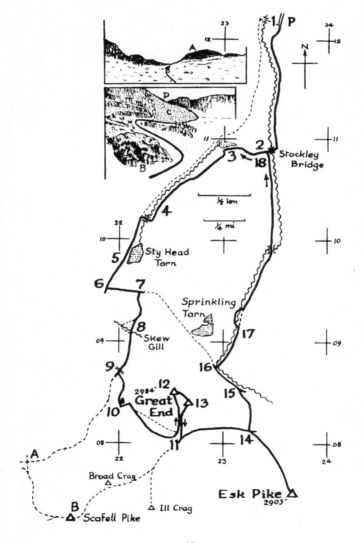

45

Scafell Pike. Those who cannot climb Scafell Pike from Wasdale can vary this route as follows: at 9 do **not** leave path. Keep on up to the col between Lingmell (R) and Scafell Pike (L). **A** Here turn L up path to summit. **B** Here go NE on clear stony path. At the large flat area (Esk Hause) you reach a path junction. **14** There turn L down path and follow 15 etc. (14.5km, 9mi.)

Two peaks seldom get a mention, as they are really part of Scafell Pike. Ill Crag (3040ft) is easily reached by a small path on the L of the path from Esk Hause to Scafell Pike. An easy flat path and a final rough bouldery rise lead to a fine summit view steeply down to the remote upper valley of Eskdale. Broad Crag (3054ft) is only 100m R of the main path mentioned above but its ascent involves an unpleasant climb over large boulders.

22. Scafell Pike from Wasdale *(11km, 6¾mi, 3300ft)* Map 89 or 90

Summary. A magnificent walk with close views of the awe-inspiring crags of both Scafell Pike, Scafell and Lingmell. Wastwater is in view more often than not. There are two tough but avoidable sections: (1) After 6 you may not fancy the rough scree ahead. If so, go L along a nearly level path to reach main path, and R up this path which soon bears R. (2) Part of the descent from Lingmell is unpleasantly steep and rough, but it is too late to turn back at that point. Cautious walkers not wishing to spoil a fine walk should retrace steps from Lingmell to the col and go R down path, later joining the ascent route at 5. Tired walkers can omit Lingmell altogether by bearing L with the main path 200m before the col.

At 11 it is quicker to go on down, saving 2km (1¼mi). The pleasant detour at an easy gradient gets you to a car park, inn, loo and packhorse bridge at Wasdale Head, before returning.

Just after passing Wastwater, turn R to car park (182075). **1** Go on (SE) from car park. **2** Over bridge and L along by stream (on your L). **3** Over bridge and up by stream (on your R). **4** Over stream and up tongue. **5** When gradient eases follow clear path just R of crest of tongue. Make for junction of 2 rough paths just below what seems to be the rim of a depression. **6** Here up grass, then up reddish scree path (not the grey scree). **7** At col (Mickledore) go L to summit. **8** Turn back 100m, then fork R

(NW) along clear path to another col. On up to top of Lingmell.
9 Turn L (W) down broad ridge. **10** After steep descent go on
over stile. **11** Soon R along gently dropping path. **12** Over stile to
bridge. On to road. **13** R along road. **14** Just past inn go L to
stream, and R to bridge. Over bridge and L along path near
stream (on your L). **15** On along road.

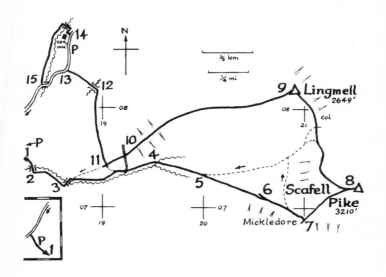

47

23. Red Pike and Pillar *(16km, 10mi, 3000ft)*

Map 89

Summary. A long but superb ridge walk with excellent views. Go a short distance N from Pillar's summit for an almost aerial view of Ennerdale and Pillar Rock. After 10 you may like to try the short cut shown on the map.

Scoat Fell can soon be reached by going on up at 7, but remember this is a long walk.

Start at car park (182075) by NE end of Wastwater. **1** Go L (SW) along road. **2** Leave road and go along clear nearly level path in bracken **3** Through gap and R up by wall (on your R). **4** Go half L away from wall along gently rising path that goes below crags (ignore path up to crags). **5** Turn L at col. **6** Along edge of crags (on your R) to Red Pike summit and on. **7** At col bear R on nearly level track with steep ground on your R. **8** After descent to col (Wind Gap) go on up to Pillar. **9** Here go R along path near old fence (on your L). **10** Zigzag eases descent. **11** Turn R at col. **12** Go R over bridge just before Wasdale Head Inn and L along path near stream (on your L). **13** On along road.

Pillar and Ennerdale from Green Gable.

48

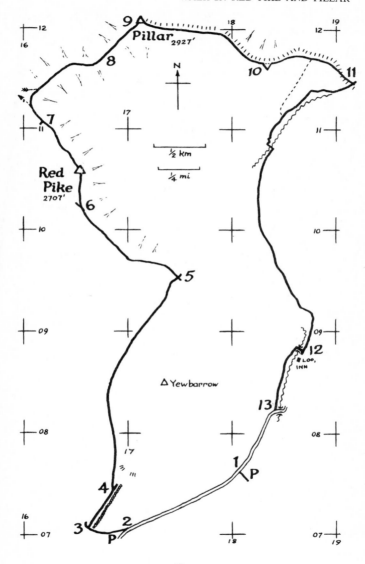

49

24. Haycock to Red Pike *(14.5km, 9mi, 3300 ft)*

Map 89

Summary. The start up the valley of Nether Beck is not the best of walks in this area, but once on the ridge the views are excellent. If you do not mind missing Haycock, it makes a better walk to stay on the path at 5 as it bears R. Soon you will reach the remote and attractive Scoat Tarn. Then on (near fence on your R) to col at 11, where you go L to Scoat Fell, or R to Red Pike. (2.5 km, 1½ mi, shorter if only Red Pike is climbed.)

Park near Netherbeck Bridge (162066) by Wastwater, 3.5km (2mi) SW of Wasdale Head. **1** Go NW up faint path 200m to good path. **2** R along this, soon with stream on your R. **3** Soon after passing wooded ravine look on up valley. Note a stream coming straight down valley side (the valley bears R there). The stream has large crag on its R. **4** When this stream is crossed stay on main valley path. It bears R and is further from the valley bottom for a while. • **5** Near fold, where path bears R, bear L off it to go up by stream (on your R) to col. **6** Here L up by wall (on your R) to Haycock. **7** Turn back to col, go through gap in wall and up by wall (now on your R). **8** At first summit go L along narrow ridge to Steeple. **9** Back along ridge and L by wall (on your R) to Scoat Fell (second summit). **10** Through wall gap and half R (SE) down to col. **11** On by steep ground on your L to Red Pike. **12** On along ridge to col. **13** Here go R on gently descending path. **14** Half R down by wall (on your L). **15** Near stream go L by it to road. R along road.

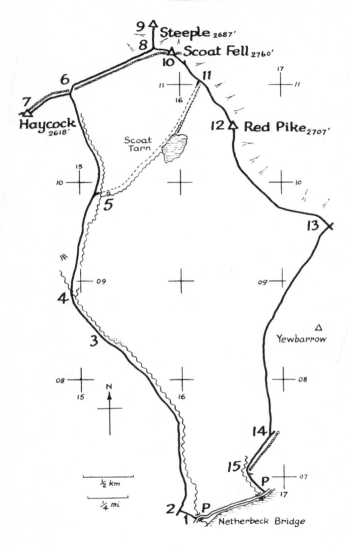

51

25. Scafell *(8km, 5mi, 3200ft)* Map 89 or 90

Summary. This is the toughest walk in the book, with scree to climb and descend, and an easy but unavoidable long scramble. The simple descent is steep enough to be rather tedious at times. For all this effort you get some magnificent rock scenery and views of Eskdale, Wastwater, etc. At 10 (the col just below the summit) you should go NE 50m to enjoy the spectacular view down Deep Gill. Foxes Tarn is the only named puddle in the district. It was a small tarn until a violent storm in 1958 reduced its status. It is not a long walk, so you could carry on past the stretcher box to Scafell Pike and back — an extra 1km (¾mi) and 500ft of climbing.

The only easy way to reach Scafell without meeting scree is to reverse the descent route: follow **1, 2,** then soon fork R (signpost 'Eskdale'). 50m after gate go half L up field to stile. **14** Over stile and R by fence. Follow path when it turns L. **13** Over stiles and up path to col. **10** Here R to summit. Return the same way.

The most exciting way up uses part of Lord's Rake: at 5, when nearing the 'rim' bear R to walk along the bottom of the crags until you reach Lord's Rake — a long bare straight gully on the R, with some scree in it. Go up this almost to top of the first rise, then step up L to a path on a shelf which takes you sensationally but safely across the crag's face to a gully (Deep Gill). Here climb very steeply up to the top. Then on to col and summit.

Just after passing Wastwater, turn R to car park (182075). **1** Go on (SE) from car park. **2** Over bridge and L along by stream (on your L). **3** Over bridge and up by stream (on your R). **4** Over stream and up tongue. **5** When gradient eases follow clear path just R of crest of tongue. Make for junction of 2 rough paths just below what seems to be the rim of a depression. **6** Here up grass, then up reddish scree path (not the grey scree). **7** At col (Mickledore) go L 50m to stretcher box, then sharp R down steep rough path. Later down grass at an easier gradient with stream on your L. **8** Look for the gully which is the first chance of getting round the crags on your R. (See small drawing.) When opposite cairn at base of gully cross 10m of boulders to reach it. (Or go down 40m and up again to get round boulders.) Scramble up the firm rock and boulders of gully (avoiding rocks made slippery by stream). Keep straight on when gradient eases. (Ignore scree shoot on your R here.) **9** At 2m high boulder in a large puddle with steeper ground behind it, go R up scree. (Soon use easier grass just R of scree, with good views of Scafell Pike.) **10** Near top follow cairns L up gentle rise to summit. **11** Return to col and go L down (NW) soon on cairned rough path with

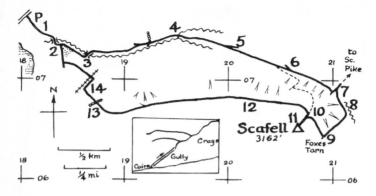

crags on your R. Bear L when crags bear L. **12** When gradient eases the path is more grassy. After path runs very close to steep ground on R keep on towards Wastwater where the steep edge and a small path bear round to the R. **13** Over stiles and on down path to fence. **14** Go R by fence and soon L over stile. Down field to track 50m to L of corner gate, then half R along track. At river go L by it and R over bridge.

Mickledore and the crags of Scafell.

53

26. Crinkle Crags *(12km, 7½mi, 2700ft)*

Map 89 or 90

Summary. A very fine mountain walk with varying views and impressive rock scenery along the crinkles. Some of the paths have rough patches, but that is a small price to pay. In wet seasons it may be difficult to cross the stream near 3, and The Band may have some short boggy patches. Peak baggers can go L when the gradient eases after 6 to reach Cold Pike (2259ft). If mist comes when you are among the crinkles follow the path carefully and do not attempt any short cuts.

There is very limited parking (shown on map) near the start of the walk, and some at Rossett Bridge (291061). The car park near the New Hotel adds 2½km (1½mi) to the walk.

1 At sharp bend in road (285060) near Dungeon Ghyll Old Hotel (Langdale), go W along track through Stool End Farm and on by wall (on your L). **2** On over stile. Soon pass just to R of fold. Go L over stile and R by wide stony stream. Cross stream on stones about 30m to L of large cairn on opposite bank. **3** At this cairn go half L up path towards a dip between mountain (on L) and smaller hill (on R). Where path (cairned) crosses stream higher up it is easier to stay on grassy path (stream on your R) until it rejoins main path. **4** On over nearly level ground. **5** Cross stream at top of small ravine and follow main path near larger ravine

Bowfell from Crinkle Crags.

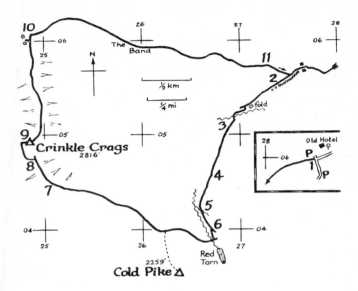

(on your R). **6** Soon fork R to a T junction. Here R along clear path. **7** Follow cairned path over first 'crinkle'. **8** At col go L along cairned path that soon bears R and climbs. After short steep section go R to follow cairns to summit. **9** Go half L (NE) along cairned path over other 'crinkles'. **10** Near Three Tarns go R down rough path starting at foot of rise to Bowfell. It goes down a broad ridge ('The Band'). **11** Over stile and bear R to go down to farm by wall (on your R).

27. Bowfell *(13km, 8mi, 2900ft)*   Map 89 or 90

Summary. This fine circuit of the head of Langdale climbs 'The Band', gives a close look at some of the magnificent crags of Bowfell and later of the dark waters of Angle Tarn sheltering beneath more of Bowfell's outcrops. Instead of the tedious descent by Rossett Gill, the walk stays high along a little walked ridge, with lovely Langdale far below it, before using the Stake Pass path for a smooth descent. (This adds some distance but is well worth it.) If you want to use the much rougher Rossett Gill path keep on down at 10 and look out for zigzags. In wet season The Band may have some short boggy sections. The going is mostly easy with a few rough or steep sections.

Keeping on at 8 will get you to Esk Pike and back for an extra 1km (¾mi).

There is very limited parking (shown on map) near the start, and some at Rossett Bridge (291061). The car park near the New Hotel adds 2½km (1½mi) to the walk.

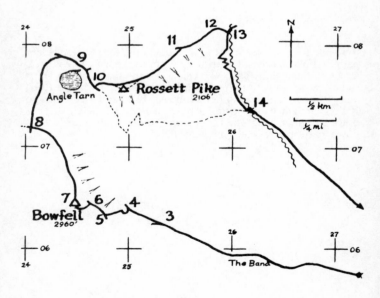

1 At sharp bend in road (285060) near Dungeon Ghyll Old Hotel (Langdale), go W along track through Stool End Farm and on by wall (on your R). **2** At top of rise fork half R up stony path up ridge (path is mainly to L of top of ridge). **3** When path becomes nearly level watch for cairn marking fork. Fork R up the smaller path which aims towards Bowfell. **4** At top of steep rise note the path goes on roughly level along the craggy hillside. Retrace steps 10m and turn half R up cairned path that bears R. When that level path is seen again, turn L with the cairns. The path goes along top of large flat rock slab. Keep on when slab ends. **5** Soon half R up large rough path. (Easier grass just to R.) When gradient eases follow cairns across shelf. **6** About 100m past huge flat rock slab on R, go L up to rocky summit. **7** Follow path and cairns roughly N, at first towards a lower summit. Bear L with the path before reaching this summit. **8** 30m before col go R on cairned path. It crosses stream and bears R to Angle Tarn. **9** Pass tarn and go up to top of rise. **10** Here go L on path. (Rossett Pike can be reached by a short detour to R). It soon gently descends with valley views on R. Later it passes just to the L of a boggy area. **11** When another path is met go half R along it. **12** After a grassy shelf the path bears R and becomes rough for a bit until a path is met by stream. **13** Here go R down this path with stream on your L. Watch for and use the mostly grassy zigzags. **14** At bottom cross bridge and go R along path. **15** On over stile past hotel and R to road.

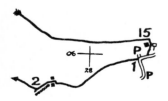

28. The Langdale Pikes *(9km, 5½mi, 2700ft).*

Map 89 or 90

Summary. Not quite up to 2500ft but too good to miss. It looks like a short walk but takes longer than expected. Some paths in this area are very rough, but this tour picks those which are easier on the feet where possible. The worst section is the rough rather tedious descent to Stickle Tarn. A path to Pike How is used to give fine views of Mill Gill. Peak baggers can visit the rather boring and hardly detectable 'mountain' called Thunacar Knott, High Raise (which at just 2500ft is left out of this book of *over* 2500ft peaks) and Sergeant Man. Not recommended.

Park in Langdale Valley near Dungeon Ghyll New Hotel (296064). **1** Go along drive past hotel to gate. Here go on 50m, then go two thirds L through wall gap. On up, soon with wall on your L. **2** Through farm gate and half R up by wall. **3** Over stile and half L over stream. Climb at first between wall and stream. **4** Later follow main cairned path as it goes sharp R, then L. **5** At large grassy area follow cairned path to red scree path (at L of the rocky tops in view). Up red path. **6** After path becomes level go L along path that runs just under Loft Crag. Soon go L up scree and R to top of Loft Crag. **7** On to the obvious Pike o' Stickle summit. **8** Retrace steps to 6, but save energy by using path that passes just L of Loft Crag. Here go L down to stream (skirting bog on your L). **9** Over stream, up 20m to path and L along it for 100m. **10** R up rough path to Harrison Stickle. **11** From its N cairn go 20m towards Pike o' Stickle (W), then R along path to cairn on col. Here go R down 50m and L (just before ground steepens) to cairn showing start of cairned path starting just R of rocky mound. Follow this nearly level path to wall gap and up to Pavey Ark. **12** Back through wall and R by it, soon reaching rough wide path down. (At first, L side of path if firmer, then R side.) **13** Over stream and R along path to Stickle Tarn. **14** Cross dam and go L to top of rise. Here R along nearly level path that bears L and descends to reach ridge just above Pike How. **15** Just before path bears R to skirt Pike How, fork half R down smoother path. At cairn avoid rough path by going half R along grassy path in bracken. It rejoins main path later. **16** Where path widens follow cairns down its L side. **17** At wall go sharp L to view waterfall (or go R by wall for quick return). Then go steeply down to path by stream. Back down, with stream on your L.

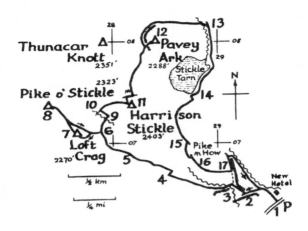

The Langdale Pikes from Lingmoor Fell.

29. Coniston Old Man and Dow Crag
(10km, 6¼mi, 2300ft)

Map 96

Summary. A fine walk with very varied scenes including the magnificent rocks of Dow Crag towering over Goat's Water. The route up Coniston Old Man is more interesting and less populated than the 'tourist' route (shown dotted on map) through unsightly mines. In mist this tourist route is an easy-to-follow return path from Coniston Old Man. (It is steep at first.) At 10, a col, turn L for an easy 'escape' route past Goat's Water (2km, 1¼mi shorter).

If you start walking from Coniston the walk is 3km (2mi) longer.

100m S of bridge at Coniston village leave A593 and go R up hill, then L up to end of surfaced section of Walna Scar Road (288971). Park here. **1** On along track until just past steep mine road on your R. **2** Here turn R up path by stream (on your R). Climb cairned path that passes to L of spoil heap. **3** At last it becomes level by old wire fence along quarry top. **4** Just as path starts to go gently down, go sharp L on cairned path. **5** Path and cairns bear R. **6** Soon after path bears L you meet the 'tourist' path and see Low Water below. Here go L to summit. **7** Bear R along edge of steep ground. When path stops being rocky go on to bottom of shallow depression. **8** Here turn L down line of cairns to clear path. **9** Here bear R down this path, which soon bears L to col. **10** On up path, never far from steep ground on your L. **11** On down from summit, still by steep ground. **12** Pass Blind Tarn below your L and up to Brown Pike. **13** Here go half R down path to col. **14** L along track. **15** Over Cove Bridge. **16** On over cross track.

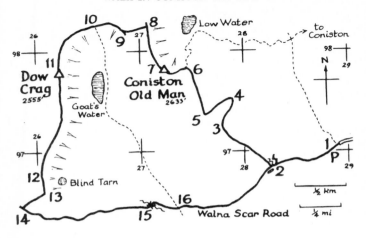

Goat's Water.

30. Wetherlam to Brim Fell *(15.5km, 9¾mi, 3900ft)*

Maps 96; 89 or 90

Summary. Another splendid horseshoe. The start is sylvan, soon reaching a fine waterfall. Then come extensive copper mines before the ridge to Wetherlam. The rocky ridge climb to Swirl How is easy and very enjoyable. Then down a superb ridge with easy walking, leaving it at Brim Fell to reach the intensely blue Low Water.

If a mist appears at 8 go L (S) down path to Levers Water and on. If it appears on Brim Fell it is better to keep on along the ridge to Coniston Old Man and bear L to join the path down to Low Water. (You could do this in fine weather, but this path is steep and tedious to descend.) Expect a few wettish patches at 5 after rain.

The visit to Grey Friar has nothing special to offer, and can be left out to save 1.5km (1mi). It should not be attempted in a mist. Even then there is more than the average amount of climbing involved on this walk, so you may wish to leave out Great Carrs as well (reducing height climbed to 3200ft).

100m S of bridge at Coniston village leave A593 and go R 150m to top of hill. Park here (300976). **1** Along signposted path by Sun Hotel. Over stream and on. Over bridge, soon with stream on your R. **2** Over bridge and L. **3** Fork R after last waterfall. Fork R just before cottages. **4** Go sharp R above cottages. Soon L on smaller path just before quarry. (This path is seen bearing L and gently rising in bracken.) **5** After path bears R it levels, with marsh on your L. Soon turn L on path by cairn. (At first it is a little vague, but soon clear and cairned.) **6** At ridge turn R by large cairn and follow clear path to top of Wetherlam. **7** Turn L (W) to path with steep ground on your R. **8** At col go on up to top of Swirl How. **9** Bear R with crags on your R to top of Great Carrs. **10** If not visiting Grey Friar return to Swirl How. For Grey Friar go WSW to col and on to summit; back to col and ESE to Swirl How. **11** At Swirl How turn R(S) down ridge with steep ground on your L. **12** Brim Fell (flat grassy top with cairn) is reached after a long gentle climb. To leave it go sharp L (NE), gently to descend a side ridge (no path). Go towards small notch (X in the drawing) at the top of a slight rise. Go on down a little R of notch, to reach a col (with Levers Water in view below L). **13** Here go R along small path towards Low Water. Cairn shows path passes just R of rocks. **14** On past Low Water (on your R) and L down track. **15** After leaving mines watch for track and path on the L of your track where it turns R (and then stays fairly straight). Here go on down path. (Or you can stay on mine track and turn L at the Walna Scar Road.)

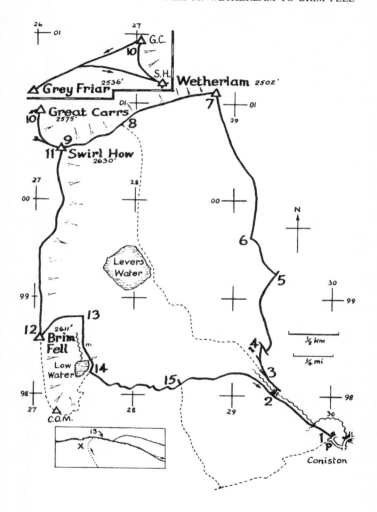

Index to places

(References are to the walk number.)

Set in 9 point Times roman and printed in Great Britain by C. I. Thomas & Sons (Haverfordwest) Ltd, Press Buildings, Merlins Bridge, Haverfordwest, Dyfed.